VEDIC
HYMNS

by

Unknown Authors

Translation by F. Max Müller.

Translation by F. Max Müller

ISBN-13:
978-1500892760

ISBN-10:
1500892769

Contents

Translation by F. Max Müller

INTRODUCTION

The Vedic Hymns are among the most interesting portions of Hindoo literature. In form and spirit they resemble both the poems of the Hebrew psalter and the lyrics of Pindar. They deal with the most elemental religious conceptions and are full of the imagery of nature. It would be absurd to deny to very many of them the possession of the truest poetic inspiration. The scenery of the Himalayas, ice and snow, storm and tempest, lend their majesty to the strains of the Vedic poet. He describes the storm sweeping over the white-crested mountains till the earth, like a hoary king, trembles with fear. The Maruts, or storm-gods, are terrible, glorious, musical, riding on strong-hoofed, never-wearying steeds. There is something Homeric, Pindaric in these epithets. Yet Soma and Rudra are addressed, though they wield sharp weapons; and sharp bolts, i.e., those of the lightning, are spoken of as kind friends. "Deliver us," says the poet, "from the snare of Varuna, and guard us, as kind-hearted gods." One of the most remarkable of these hymns is that addressed to the Unknown God. The poet says: "In the beginning there arose the Golden Child. As soon as he was born he alone was the lord of all that is. He established the earth and this heaven." The hymn consists of ten stanzas, in which the Deity is celebrated as the maker of the snowy mountains, the sea and the distant river, who made fast the awful heaven, He who alone is God above all gods, before whom heaven and earth stand trembling in their mind. Each stanza concludes with the refrain, "Who is the God to whom we shall offer sacrifice?"

We have in this hymn a most sublime conception of the Supreme Being, and while there are many Vedic hymns whose tone is pantheistic and seems to imply that the wild forces of nature are Gods who rule the world, this hymn to the Unknown God is as purely monotheistic as a psalm of David, and shows a spirit of religious awe as profound as any we find in the Hebrew Scriptures.

It is very difficult to arrive at the true date of the Vedas. The word Veda means knowledge, and is applied to unwritten literature. The Vedas are therefore the oldest Sanscrit writings which exist, and stand in the same class with regard to Hindoo literature as Homer does with regard to Greek literature. Probably the earliest Vedas were recited a thousand years before Christ, while the more recent of the hymns date about five hundred before Christ. We must therefore consider them to be the most primitive form of Aryan poetry in existence.

There is in the West a misunderstanding as to the exact meaning of "Vedic" and "Sanscrit"; for the latter is often used as if it were synonymous with Indian; whereas, only the later Indian literature can be classed under that head, and "Vedic" is often used to indicate only the Vedic Hymns, whereas it really denotes Hymns, Bráhmanas, Upanishads, and Sutras; in fact, all literature which orthodox Hindoos regard as sacred. The correct distinction then between the Vedic and the Sanscrit writings is that of holy writ and profane literature.

E.W.

VEDIC HYMNS

TO THE UNKNOWN GOD

In the beginning there arose the Golden Child. As soon as born, he alone was the lord of all that is. He established the earth and this heaven:—Who is the God to whom we shall offer sacrifice?

He who gives breath, he who gives strength, whose command all the bright gods revere, whose shadow is immortality, whose shadow is death:—Who is the God to whom we shall offer sacrifice?

He who through his might became the sole king of the breathing and twinkling world, who governs all this, man and beast:—Who is the God to whom we shall offer sacrifice?

He through whose might these snowy mountains are, and the sea, they say, with the distant river; he of whom these regions are indeed the two arms:—Who is the God to whom we shall offer sacrifice?

He through whom the awful heaven and the earth were made fast, he through whom the ether was established, and the firmament; he who measured the air in the sky:—Who is the God to whom we shall offer sacrifice?

He to whom heaven and earth, standing firm by his will, look up, trembling in their mind; he over whom the risen sun shines forth:—Who is the God to whom we shall offer sacrifice?

When the great waters went everywhere, holding the germ, and generating light, then there arose from them the breath of the gods:—Who is the God to whom we shall offer sacrifice?

He who by his might looked even over the waters which held power and generated the sacrifice, he who alone is God above all gods:—Who is the God to whom we shall offer sacrifice?

May he not hurt us, he who is the begetter of the earth, or he, the righteous, who begat the heaven; he who also begat the bright and mighty waters:—Who is the God to whom we shall offer sacrifice?

Pragâpati, no other than thou embraces all these created things. May that be ours which we desire when sacrificing to thee: may we be lords of wealth!

TO THE MARUTS[1]

I

Come hither, Maruts, on your chariots charged with lightning, resounding with beautiful songs, stored with spears, and winged with horses! Fly to us like birds, with your best food, you mighty ones! They come gloriously on their red, or, it may be, on their tawny horses which hasten their chariots. He who holds the axe is brilliant like gold;—with the tire of the chariot they have struck the earth. On your bodies there are daggers for beauty; may they stir up our minds as they stir up the forests. For yourselves, O well-born Maruts, the vigorous among you shake the stone for distilling Soma. Days went round you and came back, O hawks, back to this prayer, and to this sacred rite; the Gotamas making prayer with songs, pushed up the lid of the cloud to drink. No such hymn was ever known as this which Gotama sounded for you, O Maruts, when he saw you on golden wheels, wild boars rushing about with iron tusks. This comforting speech rushes sounding towards you, like the speech of a suppliant: it rushed freely from our hands as our speeches are wont to do.

II

Let us now proclaim for the robust host, for the herald of the powerful Indra, their ancient greatness! O ye strong-voiced

Translation by F. Max Müller

Maruts, you heroes, prove your powers on your march, as with a torch, as with a sword! Like parents bringing a dainty to their own son, the wild Maruts play playfully at the sacrifices. The Rudras reach the worshipper with their protection, strong in themselves, they do not fail the sacrificer. For him to whom the immortal guardians have given fulness of wealth, and who is himself a giver of oblations, the Maruts, who gladden men with the milk of rain, pour out, like friends, many clouds. You who have stirred up the clouds with might, your horses rushed forth, self-guided. All beings who dwell in houses are afraid of you, your march is brilliant with your spears thrust forth. When they whose march is terrible have caused the rocks to tremble, or when the manly Maruts have shaken the back of heaven, then every lord of the forest fears at your racing, each shrub flies out of your way, whirling like chariot-wheels. You, O terrible Maruts, whose ranks are never broken, favorably fulfil our prayer! Wherever your glory-toothed lightning bites, it crunches cattle, like a well-aimed bolt. The Maruts whose gifts are firm, whose bounties are never ceasing, who do not revile, and who are highly praised at the sacrifices, they sing their song for to drink the sweet juice: they know the first manly deeds of the hero Indra. The man whom you have guarded, O Maruts, shield him with hundredfold strongholds from injury and mischief—the man whom you, O fearful, powerful singers, protect from reproach in the prosperity of his children. On your chariots, O Maruts, there are all good things, strong weapons are piled up clashing against each other. When you are on your journeys, you carry the rings on your shoulders, and your axle turns the two wheels at once. In their manly arms there are many good things, on their chests golden chains, flaring ornaments, on their shoulders speckled deer-skins, on their fellies sharp edges; as birds spread their wings, they spread out splendors behind. They, mighty by might, all-powerful powers, visible from afar like the heavens with the stars, sweet-toned, soft-tongued singers with their mouths, the

Maruts, united with Indra, shout all around. This is your greatness, O well-born Maruts!—your bounty extends far, as the sway of Aditi. Not even Indra in his scorn can injure that bounty, on whatever man you have bestowed it for his good deeds. This is your kinship with us, O Maruts, that you, immortals, in former years have often protected the singer. Having through this prayer granted a hearing to man, all these heroes together have become well known by their valiant deeds. That we may long flourish, O Maruts, with your wealth, O ye racers, that our men may spread in the camp, therefore let me achieve the rite with these offerings. May this praise, O Maruts, this song of Mândârya, the son of Mâna, the poet, ask you with food for offspring for ourselves! May we have an invigorating autumn, with quickening rain!

III

For the manly host, the joyful, the wise, for the Maruts bring thou, O Nodhas, a pure offering. I prepare songs, like as a handy priest, wise in his mind, prepares the water, mighty at sacrifices. They are born, the tall bulls of heaven, the manly youths of Rudra, the divine, the blameless, pure, and bright like suns; scattering raindrops, full of terrible designs, like giants. The youthful Rudras, they who never grow old, the slayers of the demon, have grown irresistible like mountains. They throw down with their strength all beings, even the strongest, on earth and in heaven. They deck themselves with glittering ornaments for a marvellous show; on their chests they fastened gold chains for beauty; the spears on their shoulders pound to pieces; they were born together by themselves, the men of Dyu. They who confer power, the roarers, the devourers of foes, they made winds and lightnings by their powers. The shakers milk the heavenly udders, they sprinkle the earth all round with milk. The

Translation by F. Max Müller

bounteous Maruts pour forth water, mighty at sacrifices, the fat milk of the clouds. They seem to lead about the powerful horse, the cloud, to make it rain; they milk the thundering, unceasing spring. Mighty they are, powerful, of beautiful splendor, strong in themselves like mountains, yet swiftly gliding along;—you chew up forests, like wild elephants, when you have assumed your powers among the red flames. Like lions they roar, the wise Maruts, they are handsome like gazelles, the all-knowing. By night with their spotted rain-clouds and with their spears— lightnings—they rouse the companions together, they whose ire through strength is like the ire of serpents. You who march in companies, the friends of man, heroes, whose ire through strength is like the ire of serpents, salute heaven and earth! On the seats on your chariots, O Maruts, the lightning stands, visible like light. All-knowing, surrounded with wealth, endowed with powers, singers, men of endless prowess, armed with strong rings, they, the archers, have taken the arrow in their fists. The Maruts who with the golden tires of their wheels increase the rain, stir up the clouds like wanderers on the road. They are brisk, indefatigable, they move by themselves; they throw down what is firm, the Maruts with their brilliant spears make everything to reel. We invoke with prayer the offspring of Rudra, the brisk, the pure, the worshipful, the active. Cling for happiness-sake to the strong company of the Maruts, the chasers of the sky, the powerful, the impetuous. The mortal whom ye, Maruts, protected, he indeed surpasses people in strength through your protection. He carries off booty with his horses, treasures with his men; he acquires honorable wisdom, and he prospers. Give, O Maruts, to our lords strength glorious, invincible in battle, brilliant, wealth-acquiring, praiseworthy, known to all men. Let us foster our kith and kin during a hundred winters. Will you then, O Maruts, grant unto us wealth, durable, rich in men, defying all onslaughts?—wealth a hundred and a thousand-fold, always increasing?—May he who is rich in prayers come early and soon!

IV

Sing forth, O Kanvas, to the sportive host of your Maruts, brilliant on their chariots, and unscathed,—they who were born together, self-luminous, with the spotted deer, the spears, the daggers, the glittering ornaments. I hear their whips, almost close by, when they crack them in their hands; they gain splendor on their way. Sing forth the god-given prayer to the wild host of your Maruts, endowed with terrible vigor and strength. Celebrate the bull among the cows, for it is the sportive host of the Maruts; he grew as he tasted the rain. Who, O ye men, is the strongest among you here, ye shakers of heaven and earth, when you shake them like the hem of a garment? At your approach the son of man holds himself down; the gnarled cloud fled at your fierce anger. They at whose racings the earth, like a hoary king, trembles for fear on their ways, their birth is strong indeed: there is strength to come forth from their mother, nay, there is vigor twice enough for it. And these sons, the singers, stretched out the fences in their racings; the cows had to walk knee-deep. They cause this long and broad unceasing rain to fall on their ways. O Maruts, with such strength as yours, you have caused men to tremble, you have caused the mountains to tremble. As the Maruts pass along, they talk together on the way: does anyone hear them? Come fast on your quick steeds! there are worshippers for you among the Kanvas: may you well rejoice among them. Truly there is enough for your rejoicing. We always are their servants, that we may live even the whole of life.

V

Translation by F. Max Müller

To every sacrifice you hasten together, you accept prayer after prayer, O quick Maruts! Let me therefore bring you hither by my prayers from heaven and earth, for our welfare, and for our great protection; the shakers who were born to bring food and light, self-born and self-supported, like springs, like thousandfold waves of water, aye, visibly like unto excellent bulls, those Maruts, like Soma-drops, which squeezed from ripe stems dwell, when drunk, in the hearts of the worshipper—see how on their shoulders there clings as if a clinging wife; in their hands the quoit is held and the sword. Lightly they have come down from heaven of their own accord: Immortals, stir yourselves with the whip! The mighty Maruts on dustless paths, armed with brilliant spears, have shaken down even the strong places. O ye Maruts, who are armed with lightning-spears, who stirs you from within by himself, as the jaws are stirred by the tongue? You shake the sky, as if on the search for food; you are invoked by many, like the solar horse of the day. Where, O Maruts, is the top, where the bottom of the mighty sky where you came? When you throw down with the thunderbolt what is strong, like brittle things, you fly across the terrible sea! As your conquest is violent, splendid, terrible, full and crushing, so, O Maruts, is your gift delightful, like the largess of a liberal worshipper, wide-spreading, laughing like heavenly lightning. From the tires of their chariot-wheels streams gush forth, when they send out the voice of the clouds; the lightnings smiled upon the earth, when the Maruts shower down fatness. Prisni brought forth for the great fight the terrible train of the untiring Maruts: when fed they produced the dark cloud, and then looked about for invigorating food. May this praise, O Maruts, this song of Mândârya, the son of Mâna, the poet, ask you with food for offspring for ourselves! May we have an invigorating autumn, with quickening rain!

VI

The Maruts charged with rain, endowed with fierce force, terrible like wild beasts, blazing in their strength, brilliant like fires, and impetuous, have uncovered the rain-giving cows by blowing away the cloud. The Maruts with their rings appeared like the heavens with their stars, they shone wide like streams from clouds as soon as Rudra, the strong man, was born for you, O golden-breasted Maruts, in the bright lap of Prisni. They wash their horses like racers in the courses, they hasten with the points of the reed on their quick steeds. O golden-jawed Maruts, violently shaking your jaws, you go quick with your spotted deer, being friends of one mind. Those Maruts have grown to feed all these beings, or, it may be, they have come hither for the sake of a friend, they who always bring quickening rain. They have spotted horses, their bounties cannot be taken away, they are like headlong charioteers on their ways. O Maruts, wielding your brilliant spears, come hither on smooth roads with your fiery cows whose udders are swelling; being of one mind, like swans toward their nests, to enjoy the sweet offering. O one-minded Maruts, come to our prayers, come to our libations like Indra praised by men! Fulfil our prayer, like the udder of a barren cow, and make the prayer glorious by booty to the singer. Grant us this strong horse for our chariot, a draught that rouses our prayers, from day to day, food to the singers, and to the poet in our homesteads luck, wisdom, inviolable and invincible strength. When the gold-breasted Maruts harness the horses to their chariots, bounteous in wealth, then it is as if a cow in the folds poured out to her calf copious food, to every man who has offered libations. Whatever mortal enemy may have placed us among wolves, shield us from hurt, ye Vasus! Turn the wheels with burning heat against him, and strike down the weapon of the impious fiend, O Rudras! Your march, O Maruts, appears brilliant, whether even friends have milked the udder of Prisni, or whether, O sons of Rudra, you mean to blame him who praises you, and to weaken those who are weakening Trita, O unbeguiled heroes. We invoke you, the great Maruts, the constant wanderers, at the offering of the rapid Vishnu; holding ladles and prayerful we ask the golden-colored and exalted Maruts for glorious wealth. The Dasagvas carried on the sacrifice first; may they rouse us at the break of dawn. Like the dawn, they uncover the dark nights with the red rays, the strong ones, with their brilliant light, as with a sea of milk. With the morning clouds, as if with glittering red ornaments, these Maruts have grown great in the sacred places. Streaming down with rushing splendor, they have assumed their bright and brilliant color. Approaching them for their great protection to help us, we invoke them with this worship, they whom Trita may bring near, like the five Hotri priests for victory, descending on their chariot to help. May that grace of yours by which you help the wretched across all anguish, and by which you deliver the worshipper from the reviler, come hither, O Maruts; may your favor approach us like a cow going to her calf!

VII

I come to you with this adoration, with a hymn I implore the favor of the quick Maruts. O Maruts, you have rejoiced in it clearly, put down then all anger and unharness your horses! This reverent praise of yours, O Maruts, fashioned in the heart, has been offered by the mind, O gods! Come to it, pleased in your mind, for you give increase to our worship. May the Maruts when they have been praised be gracious to us, and likewise Indra, the best giver of happiness, when he has been praised.

May our lances through our valor stand always erect, O Maruts! I am afraid of this powerful one, and trembling in fear of Indra. For you the offerings were prepared—we have now put them away, forgive us! Thou through whom the Mânas see the mornings, whenever the eternal dawns flash forth with power, O Indra, O strong hero, grant thou glory to us with the Maruts, terrible with the terrible ones, strong and a giver of victory. O Indra, protect thou these bravest of men, let thy anger be turned away from the Maruts, for thou hast become victorious together with those brilliant heroes. May we have an invigorating autumn, with quickening rain!

VIII

O Maruts, that man in whose dwelling you drink the Soma, ye mighty sons of heaven, he indeed has the best guardians. You who are propitiated either by sacrifices or from the prayers of the sage, hear the call, O Maruts! Aye, the powerful man to whom you have granted a sage, he will live in a stable rich in cattle. On the altar of this strong man Soma is poured out in daily sacrifices; praise and joy are sung. To him let the mighty Maruts listen, to him who surpasses all men, as the flowing rain-clouds pass over the sun. For we, O Maruts, have sacrificed at many harvests, through the mercies of the storm-gods. May that mortal be blessed, O chasing Maruts, whose offerings you carry off. You take notice either of the sweat of him who praises you, ye men of true strength, or of the desire of the suppliant. O ye of true strength, make this manifest with might! strike the fiend with your lightning! Hide the hideous darkness, destroy every tusky fiend. Make the light which we long for!

IX

Endowed with exceeding vigor and power, the singers, the never flinching, the immovable, the impetuous, the most beloved and most manly, have decked themselves with their glittering ornaments, a few only, like the heavens with the stars. When you have seen your way through the clefts, like birds, O Maruts, on whatever road it be, then the clouds on your chariots trickle everywhere, and you pour out the honey-like fatness for him who praises you. At their racings the earth shakes, as if broken, when on the heavenly paths they harness their deer for victory. They the sportive, the roaring, with bright spears, the shakers of the clouds have themselves glorified their greatness. That youthful company, with their spotted horses, moves by itself; hence it exercises lordship, invested with powers. Thou indeed art true, thou searchest out sin, thou art without blemish. Therefore the manly host will help this prayer. We speak after the kind of our old father, our tongue goes forth at the sight of the Soma: when the singers had joined Indra in deed, then only they took their holy names;—these Maruts, armed with beautiful rings, obtained splendors for their glory, they obtained rays, and men to celebrate them; nay, armed with daggers, speeding along, and fearless, they found the beloved domain of the Maruts.

X

What then now? When will you take us as a dear father takes his son by both hands, O ye gods, for whom the sacred grass has been trimmed? Where now? On what errand of yours are you going, in heaven, not on earth? Where are your cows sporting? Where are your newest favors, O Maruts? Where the blessings? Where all delights? If you, sons of Prisni, were

18

mortals, and your praiser an immortal, then never should your praiser be unwelcome, like a deer in pasture grass, nor should he go on the path of Yama. Let not one sin after another, difficult to be conquered, overcome us; may it depart together with greed. Truly they are terrible and powerful; even to the desert the Rudriyas bring rain that is never dried up. The lightning lows like a cow, it follows as a mother follows after her young, when the shower of the Maruts has been let loose. Even by day the Maruts create darkness with the water-bearing cloud, when they drench the earth. Then from the shouting of the Maruts over the whole space of the earth, men reeled forward. Maruts on your strong-hoofed, never-wearying steeds go after those bright ones, which are still locked up. May your fellies be strong, the chariots, and their horses, may your reins be well-fashioned. Speak forth forever with thy voice to praise the Lord of prayer, Agni, who is like a friend, the bright one. Fashion a hymn in thy mouth! Expand like the cloud! Sing a song of praise. Worship the host of the Maruts, the terrible, the glorious, the musical. May they be magnified here among us.

XI

Let your voice-born prayers go forth to the great Vishnu, accompanied by the Maruts, Evayâmarut, and to the chasing host, adorned with good rings, the strong, in their jubilant throng, to the shouting power of the Maruts. O Maruts, you who are born great, and proclaim it yourselves by knowledge, Evayâmarut, that power of yours cannot be approached by wisdom, that power of theirs cannot be approached by gift or might; they are like unapproachable mountains. They who are heard with their voice from the high heaven, the brilliant and strong, Evayâmarut, in whose council no tyrant reigns, the rushing chariots of these roaring Maruts come forth, like fires with their own lightning. The wide-striding Vishnu strode forth from the great common seat, Evayâmarut. When he has started by himself from his own place along the ridges, O ye striving, mighty Maruts, he goes together with the heroes, conferring blessings. Impetuous, like your own shout, the strong one made everything tremble, the terrible, the wanderer, the mighty, Evayâmarut; strong with him you advanced self-luminous, with firm reins, golden colored, well armed, speeding along. Your greatness is infinite, ye Maruts, endowed with full power, may that terrible power help, Evayâmarut. In your raid you are indeed to be seen as charioteers; deliver us therefore from the enemy, like shining fires. May then these Rudras, lively like fires and with vigorous shine, help, Evayâmarut. The seat of the earth is stretched out far and wide, when the hosts of these faultless Maruts come quickly to the races. Come kindly on your path, O Maruts, listen to the call of him who praises you, Evayâmarut. Confidants of the great Vishnu, may you together, like charioteers, keep all hateful things far, by your wonderful skill. Come zealously to our sacrifice, ye worshipful, hear our guileless call, Evayâmarut. Like the oldest mountains in the sky, O wise guardians, prove yourselves for him irresistible to the enemy.

XII

O Syâvâsva, sing boldly with the Maruts, the singers who, worthy themselves of sacrifice, rejoice in their guileless glory according to their nature. They are indeed boldly the friends of strong power; they on their march protect all who by themselves are full of daring. Like rushing bulls, these Maruts spring over the dark cows, and then we perceive the might of the Maruts in heaven and on earth. Let us boldly offer praise and sacrifice to your Maruts, to all them who protect the generation of men, who protect the mortal from injury. They who are worthy, bounteous, men of perfect strength, to those heavenly Maruts who are worthy of sacrifice, praise the sacrifice! The tall men, coming near with their bright chains, and their weapon, have hurled forth their spears. Behind these Maruts there came by itself the splendor of heaven, like laughing lightnings. Those who have grown up on earth, or in the wide sky, or in the realm of the rivers, or in the abode of the great heaven, praise that host of the Maruts, endowed with true strength and boldness, whether those rushing heroes have by themselves harnessed their horses for triumph, or whether these brilliant Maruts have in the speckled cloud clothed themselves in wool, or whether by their strength they cut the mountain asunder with the tire of their chariot; call them comers, or goers, or enterers, or followers, under all these names, they watch on the straw for my sacrifice. The men watch, and their steeds watch. Then, so brilliant are their forms to be soon, that people say, Look at the strangers! In measured steps and wildly shouting the gleemen have danced towards the cloud. They who appeared one by one like thieves, were helpers to me to see the light. Worship, therefore, O seer, that host of Maruts, and keep and delight them with your voice, they who are themselves wise poets, tall heroes armed with lightning-spears. Approach, O seer, the host of Maruts, as a woman approaches a friend, for a gift; and you, Maruts, bold in your strength, hasten hither, even from heaven, when you have been praised by our hymns. If he, after perceiving them, has approached them as gods with an offering, then may he for a gift remain united with the brilliant Maruts, who by their ornaments are glorious on their march. They, the wise Maruts, the lords, who, when there was inquiry for their kindred, told me of the cow, they told me of Prisni as their mother, and of the strong Rudra as their father. The seven and seven heroes gave me each a hundred. On the

Translation by F. Max Müller

Yamunâ I clear off glorious wealth in cows, I clear wealth in horses.

XIII

Those who glance forth like wives and yoke-fellows, the powerful sons of Rudra on their way, they, the Maruts, have indeed made heaven and earth to grow; they, the strong and wild, delight in the sacrifices. When grown up, they attained to greatness; the Rudras have established their seat in the sky. While singing their song and increasing their vigor, the sons of Prisni have clothed themselves in beauty. When these sons of the cow adorn themselves with glittering ornaments, the brilliant ones put bright weapons on their bodies. They drive away every adversary; fatness streams along their paths;—when you, the powerful, who shine with your spears, shaking even what is unshakable by strength—when you, O Maruts, the manly hosts, had yoked the spotted deer, swift as thought, to your chariots;—when you had yoked the spotted deer before your chariots, hurling thunderbolt in the fight, then the streams of the red-horse rush forth: like a skin with water they water the earth. May the swiftly-gliding, swift-winged horses carry you hither! Come forth with your arms! Sit down on the grass-pile; a wide seat has been made for you. Rejoice, O Maruts, in the sweet food. Strong in themselves, they grew with might; they stepped to the firmament, they made their seat wide. When Vishnu saved the enrapturing Soma, the Maruts sat down like birds on their beloved altar. Like heroes indeed thirsting for fight they rush about; like combatants eager for glory they have striven in battles. All beings are afraid of the Maruts; they are men terrible to behold, like kings. When the clever Tvashtar had turned the well-made, golden, thousand-edged thunderbolt, Indra takes it to perform his manly deeds; he slew Vritra, he forced out the stream

22

of water. By their power they pushed the well aloft, they clove asunder the rock, however strong. Blowing forth their voice the bounteous Maruts performed, while drunk of Soma, their glorious deeds. They pushed the cloud athwart this way, they poured out the spring to the thirsty Gotama. The Maruts with beautiful splendor approach him with help, they in their own ways satisfied the desire of the sage. The shelters which you have for him who praises you, grant them threefold to the man who gives! Extend the same to us, O Maruts! Give us, ye heroes, wealth with valiant offspring!

XIV

Who are these resplendent men, dwelling together, the boys of Rudra, also with good horses? No one indeed knows their births, they alone know each other's birthplace. They plucked each other with their beaks; the hawks, rushing like the wind, strove together. A wise man understands these secrets, that Prisni, the great, bore an udder. May that clan be rich in heroes by the Maruts, always victorious, rich in manhood! They are quickest to go, most splendid with splendor, endowed with beauty, strong with strength. Strong is your strength, steadfast your powers, and thus by the Maruts is this clan mighty. Resplendent is your breath, furious are the minds of the wild host, like a shouting maniac. Keep from us entirely your flame, let not your hatred reach us here. I call on the dear names of your swift ones, so that the greedy should be satisfied, O Maruts, the well-armed, the swift, decked with beautiful chains, who themselves adorn their bodies. Bright are the libations for you, the bright ones, O Maruts, a bright sacrifice I prepare for the bright. In proper order came those who truly follow the order, the bright born, the bright, the pure. On your shoulders, O Maruts, are the rings, on your chests the golden chains are fastened; far-shining like lightnings with showers, you wield your weapons, according to your wont. Your hidden splendors come forth; spread out your powers, O racers! Accept, O Maruts, this thousandfold, domestic share, as an offering for the house-gods. If you thus listen, O Maruts, to this praise, at the invocation of the powerful sage, give him quickly a share of wealth in plentiful offspring, which no selfish enemy shall be able to hurt. The Maruts, who are fleet like racers, the manly youths, shone like Yakshas; they are beautiful like boys standing round the hearth, they play about like calves who are still sucking. May the bounteous Maruts be gracious to us, opening up to us the firm heaven and earth. May that bolt of yours which kills cattle and men be far from us! Incline to us, O Vasus, with your favors. The Hotri priest calls on you again and again, sitting down and praising your common gift, O Maruts. O strong ones, he who is the guardian of so much wealth, he calls on you with praises, free from guile. These Maruts stop the swift, they bend strength by strength, they ward off the curse of the plotter, and turn their heavy hatred on the enemy. These Maruts stir up even the sluggard, even the vagrant, as the gods pleased. O strong ones, drive away the darkness, and grant us all our kith and kin. May we not fall away from your bounty, O Maruts, may we not stay behind, O charioteers, in the distribution of your gifts. Let us share in the brilliant wealth, the well-acquired, that belongs to you, O strong ones. When valiant men fiercely fight together, for rivers, plants, and houses, then, O Maruts, sons of Rudra, be in battles our protectors from the enemy. O Maruts, you have valued the praises which our fathers have formerly recited to you; with the Maruts the victor is terrible in battle, with the Maruts alone the racer wins the prize. O Maruts, may we have a strong son, who is lord among men, a ruler, through whom we may cross the waters to dwell in safety, and then obtain our own home for you. May Indra then, Varuna, Mitra, Agni, the waters, the plants, the trees of the forest be pleased with us. Let us be in the keeping, in the lap of the Maruts; protect us always with your favors.

XV

Sing to the company of the Maruts, growing up together, the strong among the divine host: they stir heaven and earth by their might, they mount up to the firmament from the abyss of Nirriti. Even your birth was with fire and fury, O Maruts! You, terrible, wrathful, never tiring! You who stand forth with might and strength; everyone who sees the sun, fears at your coming. Grant mighty strength to our lords, if the Maruts are pleased with our praise. As a trodden path furthers a man, may they further us; help us with your brilliant favors. Favored by you, O Maruts, a wise man wins a hundred, favored by you a strong racer wins a thousand, favored by you a king also kills his enemy: may that gift of yours prevail, O ye shakers. I invite these bounteous sons of Rudra, will these Maruts turn again to us? Whatever they hated secretly or openly, that sin we pray the swift ones to forgive. This praise of our lords has been spoken: may the Maruts be pleased with this hymn. Keep far from us, O strong ones, all hatred, protect us always with your favors!

XVI

Come hither, do not fail, when you march forward! Do not stay away, O united friends, you who can bend even what is firm. O Maruts, Ribhukshans, come hither on your flaming strong fellies, O Rudras, come to us to-day with food, you much-desired ones, come to the sacrifice, you friends of the Sobharis. For we know indeed the terrible strength of the sons of Rudra, of the vigorous Maruts, the liberal givers of rain. The clouds were scattered, but the monster remained, heaven and earth were joined together. O you who are armed with bright rings, the tracts of the sky expanded, whenever you stir, radiant with your own splendor. Even things that cannot be thrown down resound at your race, the mountains, the lord of the forest—the earth quivers on your marches. The upper sky makes wide room, to let your violence pass, O Maruts, when these strong-armed heroes display their energies in their own bodies. According to their wont these men, exceeding terrible, impetuous, with strong and unbending forms, bring with them beautiful light. The arrow of the Sobharis is shot from the bowstrings at the golden chest on the chariot of the Maruts. They, the kindred of the cow, the well-born, should enjoy their food, the great ones should help us. Bring forward, O strongly-anointed priests, your libations to the strong host of the Maruts, the strongly advancing. O Maruts, O heroes, come quickly hither, like winged hawks, on your chariot with strong horses, of strong shape, with strong naves, to enjoy our libations. Their anointing is the same, the golden chains shine on their arms, their spears sparkle. These strong, manly, strong-armed Maruts, do not strive among themselves; firm are the bows, the weapons on your chariot, and on your faces are splendors. They whose terrible name, wide-spreading like the ocean, is the one of all that is of use, whose strength is like the vigor of their father, worship these Maruts, and praise them! Of these shouters, as of moving spokes, no one is the last; this is theirs by gift, by greatness is it theirs. Happy is he who was under your protection, O Maruts, in former mornings, or who may be so even now. Or he, O men, whose libations you went to enjoy; that mighty one, O shakers, will obtain your favors with brilliant riches and booty. As the sons of Rudra, the servants of the divine Dyu, will it, O youths, so shall it be. Whatever liberal givers may worship the Maruts, and move about together as generous benefactors, even from them turn towards us with a kinder heart, you youths! O Sobhari, call loud with your newest song the young, strong, and pure Maruts, as the plougher calls the cows. Worship the Maruts with a song, they who are strong like a boxer, called in to assist those who call for him in all fights; worship them the most glorious, like bright-shining bulls. Yes, O united friends, kindred, O Maruts, by a common birth, the oxen lick one another's humps. O ye dancers, with golden ornaments on your chests, even a mortal comes to ask for your brotherhood; take care of us, ye Maruts, for your friendship lasts forever. O bounteous Maruts, bring us some of your Marut-medicine, you friends, and steeds. With the favors whereby you favor the Sindhu, whereby you save, whereby you help Krivi, with those propitious favors be our delight, O delightful ones, ye who never hate your followers. O Maruts, for whom we have prepared good altars, whatever medicine there is on the Sindhu, on the Asiknî, in the seas, on the mountains, seeing it, you carry it all on your bodies. Bless us with it! Down to the earth, O Maruts, with what hurts our sick one—straighten what is crooked!

XVII

Full of devotion like priests with their prayers, wealthy like pious men, who please the gods with their offerings, beautiful to behold like brilliant kings, without a blemish like the youths of our hamlets—they who are gold-breasted like Agni with his splendor, quick to help like self-harnessed winds, good leaders like the oldest experts, they are to the righteous man like Somas, that yield the best protection. They who are roaring and hasting like winds, brilliant like the tongues of fires, powerful like mailed soldiers, full of blessings like the prayers of our fathers, who hold together like the spokes of chariot-wheels, who glance forward like victorious heroes, who scatter ghrita like wooing youths, who chant beautifully like singers, intoning a hymn of praise, who are swift like the best of horses, who are bounteous like lords of chariots on a suit, who are hastening on like water with downward floods, who are like the manifold Angiras with their numerous songs. These noble sons of Sindhu are like grinding-stones, they are always like Soma-stones, tearing everything to pieces; these sons of a good mother are like playful children, they are by their glare like a great troop on its march. Illumining the sacrifice like the rays of the dawn, they shone forth in their ornaments like triumphant warriors; the Maruts with bright spears seem like running rivers, from afar they measure many miles. O gods, make us happy and rich, prospering us, your praisers, O Maruts! Remember our praise and our friendship, for from of old there are always with you gifts of treasures.

XVIII

O Indra, a thousand have been thy helps accorded to us, a thousand, O driver of the bays, have been thy most delightful viands. May thousands of treasures richly to enjoy, may goods come to us a thousandfold. May the Maruts come towards us with their aids, the mighty ones, or with their best aids from the great heaven, now that their furthest steeds have rushed forth on the distant shore of the sea; there clings to the Maruts one who moves in secret, like a man's wife,[2] and who is like a spear carried behind, well grasped, resplendent, gold-adorned; there is also with them Vâk,[3] like unto a courtly, eloquent woman. Far away the brilliant, untiring Maruts cling to their young maid, as if she belonged to them all; but the terrible ones did not drive away Rodasi, for they wished her to grow their friend. When the divine Rodasi with dishevelled locks, the manly-minded, wished to follow them, she went, like Sûryâ,[4] to the chariot of her servant, with terrible look, as with the pace of a cloud. As soon as the poet with the libations, O Maruts, had sung his song at the sacrifice, pouring out Soma, the youthful men placed the young maid in their chariot as their companion for victory, mighty in assemblies. I praise what is the praiseworthy true greatness of those Maruts, that the manly-minded, proud, and strong one drives with them towards the blessed mothers. They protect Mitra and Varuna from the unspeakable, and Aryaman also finds out the infamous. Even what is firm and unshakable is being shaken; but he who dispenses treasures, O Maruts, has grown in strength. No people indeed, whether near to us, or from afar, have ever found the end of your strength, O Maruts! The Maruts, strong in daring strength, have, like the sea, boldly surrounded their haters. May we to-day, may we tomorrow in battle be called the most beloved of Indra. We were so formerly, may we truly be so day by day, and may the lord of the Maruts be with us. May this praise, O Maruts, this song of Mândârya, the son of Mâna, the poet, ask you with food for offspring for ourselves! May we have an invigorating autumn, with quickening rain!

XIX

Who knows their birth? or who was of yore in the favor of the Maruts, when they harnessed the spotted deer? Who has heard them when they had mounted their chariots, how they went forth? For the sake of what liberal giver did they run, and their comrades followed, as streams of rain filled with food? They themselves said to me when day by day they came to the feast with their birds: they are manly youths and blameless; seeing them, praise them thus; they who shine by themselves in their ornaments, their daggers, their garlands, their golden chains, their rings, going on their chariots and on dry land. O Maruts, givers of quickening rain, I am made to rejoice, following after your chariots, as after days going with rain. The bucket which the bounteous heroes shook down from heaven for their worshipper, that cloud they send along heaven and earth, and showers follow on the dry land. The rivers having pierced the air with a rush of water, went forth like milk-cows; when your spotted deer roll about like horses that have hasted to the resting-place on their road. Come hither, O Maruts, from heaven, from the sky, even from near; do not go far away! Let not the Rasâ, the Anitabhâ, the Kubhâ, the Krumu, let not the Sindhu delay you! Let not the marshy Sarayu prevent you! May your favor be with us alone! The showers come forth after the host of your chariots, after the terrible Marut-host of the ever-youthful heroes. Let us then follow with our praises and our prayers each host of yours, each troop, each company. To what well-born generous worshipper have the Maruts gone to-day on that march, on which you bring to kith and kin the never-failing seed of corn? Give us that for which we ask you, wealth and everlasting happiness! Let us safely pass through our revilers, leaving behind the unspeakable and the enemies. Let us be with you when in the morning you shower down health, wealth, water, and medicine, O Maruts! That mortal, O men, O Maruts, whom you protect, may well be always beloved by the gods, and rich in valiant offspring. May we be such! Praise the liberal Maruts, and may they delight on the path of this man here who praises them, like cows in fodder. When they go, call after them as for old friends, praise them who love you, with your song!

XX

You have fashioned this speech for the brilliant Marut-host which shakes the mountains: celebrate then the great manhood in honor of that host who praises the warm milk of the sacrifice, and sacrifices on the height of heaven, whose glory is brilliant. O Maruts, your powerful men came forth searching for water, invigorating, harnessing their horses, swarming around. When they aim with the lightning, Trita shouts, and the waters murmur, running around on their course. These Maruts are men brilliant with lightning, they shoot with thunderbolts, they blaze with the wind, they shake the mountains, and suddenly, when wishing to give water, they whirl the hail; they have thundering strength, they are robust, they are ever-powerful. When you drive forth the nights, O Rudras, the days, O powerful men, the sky, the mists, ye shakers, the plains, like ships, and the strongholds, O Maruts, you suffer nowhere. That strength of yours, O Maruts, that greatness extended as far as the sun extends its daily course, when you, like your deer on their march, went down to the western mountain with untouched splendor. Your host, O Maruts, shone forth when, O sages, you strip, like a caterpillar, the waving tree. Conduct then, O friends, our service to a good end, as the eye conducts the man in walking. That man, O Maruts, is not overpowered, he is not killed, he does not fail, he does not shake, he does not drop, his goods do not perish, nor his protections, if you lead him rightly, whether he be a seer or a king. The men with their steeds, like conquerors of clans, like Aryaman, the Maruts, carrying waterskins, fill the well; when the strong ones roar, they moisten the earth with the juice of sweetness. When the Maruts come forth this earth bows, the heaven bows, the paths in the sky bow, and the cloud-mountains with their quickening rain. When you rejoice at sunrise, O Maruts, toiling together, men of sunlight, men of heaven, your horses never tire in running, and you quickly reach the end of your journey. On your shoulders are the spears, on your feet rings, on your chests golden chains, O Maruts, on your chariot gems; fiery lightnings in your fists, and golden headbands tied round your heads. O Maruts, you shake the red apple from the firmament, whose splendor no enemy can touch; the hamlets bowed when the Maruts blazed, and the pious people intoned their far-reaching shout. O wise Maruts, let us carry off the wealth of food which you have bestowed on us; give us, O

Maruts, such thousandfold wealth as never fails, like the star Tishya from heaven! O Maruts, you protect our wealth of excellent men, and the seer, clever in song; you give to the warrior a strong horse, you make the king to be obeyed. O you who are quickly ready to help, I implore you for wealth whereby we may overshadow all men, like the sky. O Maruts, be pleased with this word of mine, and let us speed by its speed over a hundred winters!

XXI

The chasing Maruts with gleaming spears, the golden-breasted, have gained great strength, they move along on quick, well-broken horses;—when they went in triumph, the chariots followed. You have yourselves, you know, acquired power; you shine bright and wide, you great ones. They have even measured the sky with their strength;—when they went in triumph, the chariots followed. The strong heroes, born together, and nourished together, have further grown to real beauty. They shine brilliantly like the rays of the sun;—when they went in triumph, the chariots followed. Your greatness, O Maruts, is to be honored, it is to be yearned for like the sight of the sun. Place us also in immortality;—when they went in triumph, the chariots followed. O Maruts, you raise the rain from the sea, and rain it down, O yeomen! Your milch-cows, O destroyers, are never destroyed;—when they went in triumph, the chariots followed. When you have joined the deer as horses to the shafts, and have clothed yourselves in golden garments, then, O Maruts, you scatter all enemies;—when they went in triumph, the chariots followed. Not mountains, not rivers have kept you back, wherever you see, O Maruts, there you go. You go even round heaven and earth;—when they went in triumph, the chariots followed. Be it old, O Maruts, or be it new, be it spoken, O

Vasus, or be it recited, you take cognizance of it all;—when they went in triumph, the chariots followed. Have mercy on us, O Maruts, do not strike us, extend to us your manifold protection. Do remember the praise, the friendship;—when they went in triumph, the chariots followed. Lead us, O Maruts, towards greater wealth, and out of tribulations, when you have been praised. O worshipful Maruts, accept our offering, and let us be lords of treasures!

XXII

O Agni, on to the strong host of the Maruts, bedecked with golden chains and ornaments. To-day I call the folk of the Maruts down from the light of heaven. As thou, Agni, thinkest in thine heart, to the same object my wishes have gone. Strengthen thou these Maruts, terrible to behold, who have come nearest to thy invocations. Like a bountiful lady, the earth comes towards us, staggering, yet rejoicing; for your onslaught, O Maruts, is vigorous, like a bear, and fearful, like a wild bull. They who by their strength disperse wildly like bulls, impatient of the yoke, they by their marches make the heavenly stone, the rocky mountain cloud to shake. Arise, for now I call with my hymns the troop of these Maruts, grown strong together, the manifold, the incomparable, as if calling a drove of bulls. Harness the red mares to the chariot, harness the ruddy horses to the chariots, harness the two bays, ready to drive in the yoke, most vehement to drive in the yoke. And this red stallion too, loudly neighing, has been placed here, beautiful to behold; may it not cause you delay on your marches, O Maruts; spur him forth on your chariots.

We call towards us the glorious chariot of the Maruts, whereon there stands also Rodasî, carrying delightful gifts, among the Maruts.

Translation by F. Max Müller

I call hither this your host, brilliant on chariots, terrible and glorious, among which she, the well-born and fortunate, the bounteous lady, is also magnified among the Maruts.

XXIII

O Rudras, joined by Indra, friends on golden chariots, come hither for our welfare! This prayer from us is acceptable to you like the springs of heaven to a thirsty soul longing for water. O you sons of Prisni, you are armed with daggers and spears, you are wise, carrying good bows and arrows and quivers, possessed of good horses and chariots. With your good weapons, O Maruts, you go to triumph! You shake the sky and the mountains for wealth to the liberal giver; the forests bend down out of your way from fear. O sons of Prisni, you rouse the earth when you, O terrible ones, have harnessed the spotted deer for triumph! The Maruts, blazing with the wind, clothed in rain, are as like one another as twins, and well adorned. They have tawny horses, and red horses, they are faultless, endowed with exceeding vigor; they are in greatness wide as the heaven. Rich in rain-drops, well adorned, bounteous, terrible to behold, of inexhaustible wealth, noble by birth, golden-breasted, these singers of the sky have obtained their immortal name. Spears are on your two shoulders, in your arms are placed strength, power, and might. Manly thoughts dwell in your heads, on your chariots are weapons, and every beauty has been laid on your bodies. O Maruts, you have given us wealth of cows, horses, chariots, and heroes, golden wealth! O men of Rudra, bestow on us great praise, and may I enjoy your divine protection! Hark, O heroes, O Maruts! Be gracious to us! You who are of great bounty, immortal, righteous, truly listening to us, poets, young, dwelling on mighty mountains, and grown mighty.

XXIV

I praise now the powerful company of these ever-young Maruts, who drive violently along with quick horses; aye, the sovereigns are lords of Amrita the immortal. The terrible company, the powerful, adorned with quoits on their hands, given to roaring, potent, dispensing treasures, they who are beneficent, infinite in greatness, praise, O poet, these men of great wealth! May your water-carriers come here to-day, all the Maruts who stir up the rain. That fire which has been lighted for you, O Maruts, accept it, O young singers! O worshipful Maruts, you create for man an active king, fashioned by Vibhvan; from you comes the man who can fight with his fist, and is quick with his arm, from you the man with good horses and valiant heroes. Like the spokes of a wheel, no one is last, like the days they are born on and on, not deficient in might. The very high sons of Prisni are full of fury, the Maruts cling firmly to their own will. When you have come forth with your speckled deer as horses on strong-fellied chariots, O Maruts, the waters gush, the forests go asunder;—let Dyu roar down, the bull of the Dawn. At their approach, even the earth opened wide, and they placed their own strength as a husband the germ. Indeed they have harnessed the winds as horses to the yoke, and the men of Rudra have changed their sweat into rain. Hark, O heroes, O Maruts! Be gracious to us! You who are of great bounty, immortal, righteous, truly listening to us, poets, young, dwelling on mighty mountains, and grown mighty.

XXV

They truly tried to make you grant them welfare. Do thou sing praises to Heaven, I offer sacrifice to the Earth. The Maruts wash their horses and race to the air, they soften their splendor by waving mists. The earth trembles with fear from their onset. She sways like a full ship, that goes rolling. The heroes who appear on their marches, visible from afar, strive together within the great sacrificial assembly. Your horn is exalted for glory, as the horns of cows; your eye is like the sun, when the mist is scattered. Like strong racers, you are beautiful, O heroes, you think of glory, like manly youths. Who could reach, O Maruts, the great wise thoughts, who the great manly deeds of you, great ones? You shake the earth like a speck of dust, when you are carried forth for granting welfare. These kinsmen are like red horses, like heroes eager for battle, and they have rushed forward to fight. They are like well-grown manly youths, and the men have grown strong, with streams of rain they dim the eye of the sun. At their outbreak there is none among them who is the eldest, or the youngest, or the middle: they have grown by their own might, these sons of Prisni, noble by birth, the boys of Dyaus; come hither to us!

Those who like birds flew with strength in rows from the ridge of the mighty heaven to its ends, their horses shook the springs of the mountain cloud, so that people on both sides knew it. May Dyaus Aditi roar for our feast, may the dew-lighted Dawns come striving together; these, the Maruts, O poet, the sons of Rudra, have shaken the heavenly bucket cloud, when they had been praised.

Footnote 1:   The Maruts are the "Storm-Gods".
Footnote 2:   The lightning.
Footnote 3:   The voice of thunder.
Footnote 4:   The dawn.

TO THE MARUTS AND INDRA

The Prologue

The sacrificer speaks:

To what splendor do the Maruts all equally cling, they who are of the same age, and dwell in the same nest? With what thoughts?—from whence are they come? Do these heroes sing forth their own strength, wishing for wealth? Whose prayers have the youths accepted? Who has turned the Maruts to his own sacrifice? By what strong desire may we arrest them, they who float through the air like hawks?

The Dialogue

The Maruts speak:

From whence, O Indra, dost thou come alone, thou who art mighty? O lord of men, what has thus happened to thee? Thou greetest us when thou comest together with us. Tell us then, thou with thy bay horses, what thou hast against us!

Indra speaks:

The sacred songs are mine, the prayers; sweet are the libations! My strength rises, my thunderbolt is hurled forth. They call for me, the hymns yearn for me. Here are my horses, they carry me hither.

The Maruts speak:

From thence, in company with our strong friends, having adorned our bodies, we now harness our fallow deer with all our might;—for, Indra, according to custom, thou hast come to be with us.

Indra speaks:

Where, O Maruts, was that custom with you, when you left me alone in the killing of Ahi? I indeed am terrible, powerful, strong,—I escaped from the blows of every enemy.

The Maruts speak:

Thou hast achieved much with us as companions. With equal valor, O hero! let us achieve then many things, O thou most powerful, O Indra! whatever we, O Maruts, wish with our mind.

Indra speaks:

I slew Vritra, O Maruts, with Indra's might, having grown powerful through my own vigor; I, who hold the thunderbolt in my arms, have made these all-brilliant waters to flow freely for man.

The Maruts speak:

Nothing, O mighty lord, is strong before thee: no one is known among the gods like unto thee. No one who is now born comes near, no one who has been born. Do what thou wilt do, thou who art grown so strong.

Indra speaks:

Almighty strength be mine alone, whatever I may do, daring in my heart; for I indeed, O Maruts, am known as terrible: of all that I threw down, I, Indra, am the lord.

O Maruts, now your praise has pleased me, the glorious hymn which you have made for me, ye men!—for me, for Indra, for the joyful hero, as friends for a friend, for your own sake, and by your own efforts.

Truly, there they are, shining towards me, bringing blameless glory, bringing food. O Maruts, wherever I have looked for you, you have appeared to me in bright splendor: appear to me also now!

The Epilogue

The sacrificer speaks:

Who has magnified you here, O Maruts? Come hither, O friends, towards your friends. Ye brilliant Maruts, welcoming these prayers, be mindful of these my rites. The wisdom of Mânya has brought us hither, that he should help as the poet helps the performer of a sacrifice: turn hither quickly! Maruts, on to the sage! the singer has recited these prayers for you. May this your praise, O Maruts, this song of Mândârya, the son of Mâna, the poet, bring offspring for ourselves with food. May we have an invigorating autumn, with quickening rain.

TO INDRA AND THE MARUTS

Those who stand around him while he moves on, harness the bright red steed; the lights in heaven shine forth. They harness to the chariot on each side his two favorite bays, the brown, the bold, who can carry the hero. Thou who createst light where there was no light, and form, O men! where there was no form, hast been born together with the dawns. Thereupon they (the Maruts), according to their wont, assumed again the form of new-born babes, taking their sacred name. Thou, O Indra, with the swift Maruts, who break even through the stronghold, hast found even in their hiding-place the bright ones. The pious singers have, after their own mind, shouted towards the giver of wealth, the great, the glorious Indra. Mayest thou, host of the Maruts, be verily seen coming together with Indra, the fearless: you are both happy-making, and of equal splendor. With the beloved hosts of Indra, with the blameless, hasting (Maruts), the sacrificer cries aloud. From yonder, O traveller, Indra, come hither, or from the light of heaven; the singers all yearn for it;— or we ask Indra for help from here, or from heaven, or from above the earth, or from the great sky.

TO AGNI AND THE MARUTS[5]

Thou art called forth to this fair sacrifice for a draught of milk; with the Maruts come hither, O Agni! No god indeed, no mortal, is beyond the might of thee, the mighty one; with the Maruts come hither, O Agni! They who know of the great sky, the Visve Devas without guile; with those Maruts come hither, O Agni! The strong ones who sing their song, unconquerable by force; with the Maruts come hither, O Agni! They who are brilliant, of terrible designs, powerful, and devourers of foes; with the Maruts come hither, O Agni! They who in heaven are enthroned as gods, in the light of the firmament; with the Maruts come hither, O Agni! They who toss the clouds across the surging sea; with the Maruts come hither, O Agni! They who shoot with their darts across the sea with might; with the Maruts come hither, O Agni! I pour out to thee for the early draught the sweet juice of Soma; with the Maruts come hither, O Agni!

Footnote 5:   Agni is the "God of Fire."

TO RUDRA[6]

We offer these prayers to Rudra, the strong, whose hair is braided, who rules over heroes that he may be a blessing to man and beast, that everything in this our village may be prosperous and free from disease. Be gracious to us, O Rudra, and give us joy, and we shall honor thee, the ruler of heroes, with worship. What health and wealth father Manu acquired by his sacrifices, may we obtain the same, O Rudra, under thy guidance. O bounteous Rudra, may we by sacrifice obtain the good-will of thee, the ruler of heroes; come to our clans, well-disposed, and, with unarmed men, we shall offer our libation to thee. We call down for our help the fierce Rudra, who fulfils our sacrifice, the swift, the wise; may he drive far away from us the anger of the gods; we desire his good-will only. We call down with worship the red boar of the sky, the god with braided hair, the blazing form; may he who carries in his hand the best medicines grant us protection, shield, and shelter! This speech is spoken for the father of the Maruts, sweeter than sweet, a joy to Rudra; grant to us also, O immortal, the food of mortals, be gracious to us and to our kith and kin! Do not slay our great or our small ones, our growing or our grown ones, our father or our mother, and do not hurt our own bodies, O Rudra! O Rudra, hurt us not in our kith and kin, nor in our own life, not in our cows, nor in our horses! Do not slay our men in thy wrath: carrying libations, we call on thee always. Like a shepherd, I have driven these praises near to thee; O father of the Maruts, grant us thy favor! For thy good-will is auspicious, and most gracious, hence we desire thy protection alone. Let thy cow-slaying and thy man-slaying be far away, and let thy favor be with us, O ruler of heroes! Be gracious to us, and bless us, O god, and then give us twofold protection. We have uttered our supplication to him, desiring his help; may Rudra with the Maruts hear our call. May Mitra, Varuna, Aditi, the River, Earth, and the Sky, grant us this!

Footnote 6: Rudra is the "Father of the Maruts."

TO RUDRA

O father of the Maruts, let thy favor come near, and do not deprive us of the sight of the sun; may the hero (Rudra) be gracious to our horse, and may we increase in offspring, O Rudra! May I attain to a hundred winters through the most

Translation by F. Max Müller

blissful medicines which thou hast given! Put away far from us all hatred, put away anguish, put away sickness in all directions! In beauty thou art the most beautiful of all that exists, O Rudra, the strongest of the strong, thou wielder of the thunderbolt! Carry us happily to the other shore of our anguish, and ward off all assaults of mischief. Let us not incense thee, O Rudra, by our worship, not by bad praise, O hero, and not by divided praise! Raise up our men by thy medicines, for I hear thou art the best of all physicians. He who is invoked by invocations and libations, may I pay off that Rudra with my hymns of praise. Let not him who is kind-hearted, who readily hears our call, the tawny, with beautiful cheeks, deliver us to this wrath! The manly hero with the Maruts has gladdened me, the suppliant, with more vigorous health. May I without mischief find shade, as if from sunshine, may I gain the favor of Rudra! O Rudra, where is thy softly stroking hand which cures and relieves? Thou, the remover of all heaven-sent mischief, wilt thou, O strong hero, bear with me? I send forth a great, great hymn of praise to the bright tawny bull. Let me reverence the fiery god with prostrations; we celebrate the flaring name of Rudra. He, the fierce god, with strong limbs, assuming many forms, the tawny Rudra, decked himself with brilliant golden ornaments. From Rudra, who is lord of this wide world, divine power will never depart. Worthily thou bearest arrows and bow, worthily, O worshipful, the golden, variegated chain; worthily thou cuttest every fiend here to pieces, for there is nothing indeed stronger than thou, O Rudra. Praise him, the famous, sitting in his chariot, the youthful, who is fierce and attacks like a terrible lion. And when thou hast been praised, O Rudra, be gracious to him who magnifies thee, and let thy armies mow down others than us! O Rudra, a boy indeed makes obeisance to his father who comes to greet him: I praise the lord of brave men, the giver of many gifts, and thou, when thou hast been praised, wilt give us thy medicines. O Maruts, those pure medicines of yours, the most beneficent and delightful, O heroes, those which Manu, our father, chose, those I crave from Rudra, as health and wealth. May the weapon of Rudra avoid us, may the great anger of the flaring one pass us by. Unstring thy strong bows for the sake of our liberal lords, O bounteous Rudra, be gracious to our kith and kin. Thus, O tawny and manly god, showing thyself, so as neither to be angry nor to kill, be mindful of our invocations, and, rich in brave sons, we shall magnify thee in the congregation.

TO AGNI AND THE MARUTS

I implore Agni, the gracious, with salutations, may he sit down here, and gather what we have made. I offer him sacrifice as with racing chariots; may I, turning to the right, accomplish this hymn to the Maruts. Those who approached on their glorious deer, on their easy chariots, the Rudras, the Maruts—through fear of you, ye terrible ones, the forests even bend down, the earth shakes, and also the mountain cloud. At your shouting, even the mountain cloud, grown large, fears, and the ridge of heaven trembles. When you play together, O Maruts, armed with spears, you run together like waters. Like rich suitors the Maruts have themselves adorned their bodies with golden ornaments; more glorious for glory, and powerful on their chariots, they have brought together splendors on their bodies. As brothers, no one being the eldest or the youngest, they have grown up together to happiness. Young is their clever father Rudra, flowing with plenty is Prisni, always kind to the Maruts. O happy Maruts, whether you are in the highest, or in the middle, or in the lowest heaven, from thence, O Rudras, or thou also, O Agni, take notice of this libation which we offer. When Agni, and you, wealthy Maruts, drive down from the higher heaven over the ridges, give then, if pleased, you roarers, O destroyers of enemies, wealth to the sacrificer who prepares Soma-juice. Agni, be pleased to drink

Soma with the brilliant Maruts, the singers, approaching in companies, with the men, who brighten and enliven everything; do this, Agni, thou who art always endowed with splendor.

TO VÂYU

Come hither, O Vâyu, thou beautiful one! These Somas are ready, drink of them, hear our call! O Vâyu, the praisers celebrate thee with hymns, they who know the feast-days, and have prepared the Soma. O Vâyu, thy satisfying stream goes to the worshipper, wide-reaching, to the Soma-draught. O Indra and Vâyu, these libations of Soma are poured out; come hither for the sake of our offerings, for the drops of Soma long for you. O Indra and Vâyu, you perceive the libations, you who are rich in booty; come then quickly hither! O Vâyu and Indra, come near to the work of the sacrificer, quick, thus is my prayer, O ye men! I call Mitra, endowed with holy strength, and Varuna, who destroys all enemies; who both fulfil a prayer accompanied by fat offerings. On the right way, O Mitra and Varuna, you have obtained great wisdom, you who increase the right and adhere to the right; These two sages, Mitra and Varuna, the mighty, wide-ruling, give us efficient strength.

TO VÂYU

O Vâyu, may the quick racers bring thee towards the offerings, to the early drink here, to the early drink of Soma! May the Dawn stand erect, approving thy mind! Come near on thy harnessed chariot to share, O Vâyu, to share in the sacrifice! May the delightful drops of Soma delight thee, the drops made by us, well-made, and heaven-directed, yes, made with milk, and heaven-directed. When his performed aids assume strength for achievement, our prayers implore the assembled steeds for gifts, yes, the prayers implore them. Vâyu yokes the two ruddy, Vâyu yokes the two red horses, Vâyu yokes to the chariot the two swift horses to draw in the yoke, the strongest to draw in the yoke. Awake Purandhi (the morning) as a lover wakes a sleeping maid, reveal heaven and earth, brighten the dawn, yes, for glory brighten the dawn. For thee the bright dawns spread out in the distance beautiful garments, in their houses, in their rays, beautiful in their new rays. To thee the juice-yielding cow pours out all treasures. Thou hast brought forth the Maruts from the flanks, yes, from the flanks of heaven. For thee the white, bright, rushing Somas, strong in raptures, have rushed to the whirl, they have rushed to the whirl of the waters. The tired hunter asks luck of thee in the chase; thou shieldest by thy power from every being, yes, thou shieldest by thy power from powerful spirits. Thou, O Vâyu, art worthy as the first before all others to drink these our Somas, thou art worthy to drink these poured-out Somas. Among the people also who invoke thee and have turned to thee, all the cows pour out the milk, they pour out butter and milk for the Soma.

INDRA AND AGASTYA: A DIALOGUE[7]

Indra: There is no such thing to-day, nor will it be so to-morrow. Who knows what strange thing this is? We must consult the thought of another, for even what we once knew seems to vanish.

Agastya: Why dost thou wish to kill us, O Indra? the Maruts are thy brothers; fare kindly with them, and do not strike us in battle.

The Maruts: O Brother Agastya, why, being a friend, dost thou despise us? We know quite well what thy mind was. Dost thou not wish to give to us?

Agastya: Let them prepare the altar, let them light the fire in front! Here we two will spread for thee the sacrifice, to be seen by the immortal.

Agastya: Thou rulest, O lord of treasures; thou, lord of friends, art the most generous. Indra, speak again with the Maruts, and then consume our offerings at the right season.

Footnote 7:   Agastya is a worshipper of Indra.

TO SOMA AND RUDRA

Soma and Rudra, may you maintain your divine dominion, and may the oblations reach you properly. Bringing the seven treasures to every house, be kind to our children and our cattle. Soma and Rudra, draw far away in every direction the disease which has entered our house. Drive far away Nirriti, and may auspicious glories belong to us! Soma and Rudra, bestow all these remedies on our bodies. Tear away and remove from us whatever evil we have committed, which clings to our bodies. Soma and Rudra, wielding sharp weapons and sharp bolts, kind friends, be gracious unto us here! Deliver us from the snare of Varuna, and guard us, as kind-hearted gods!

TO RUDRA

Offer ye these songs to Rudra whose bow is strong, whose arrows are swift, the self-dependent god, the unconquered conqueror, the intelligent, whose weapons are sharp—may he hear us! For, being the lord, he looks after what is born on earth; being the universal ruler, he looks after what is born in heaven. Protecting us, come to our protecting doors, be without illness among our people, O Rudra! May that thunderbolt of thine, which, sent from heaven, traverses the earth, pass us by! A thousand medicines are thine, O thou who art freely accessible; do not hurt us through our kith and kin! Do not strike us, O Rudra, do not forsake us! May we not be in thy way when thou rushest forth furiously. Let us have our altar and a good report among men—protect us always with your favors!

TO VÂTA

Now for the greatness of the chariot of Vâta. Its roar goes crashing and thundering. It moves touching the sky, and creating red sheens, or it goes scattering the dust of the earth. Afterwards there rise the gusts of Vâta, they go towards him, like women to a feast. The god goes with them on the same chariot, he, the king of the whole of this world. When he moves on his paths along the sky, he rests not even a single day; the friend of the waters, the first-born, the holy, where was he born, whence did he spring? The breath of the gods, the germ of the world, that god moves wherever he listeth; his roars indeed are heard, not his form—let us offer sacrifice to that Vâta!

TO VÂTA

May Vâta waft medicine, healthful, delightful to our heart; may he prolong our lives! Thou, O Vâta, art our father, and our brother, and our friend; do thou grant us to live! O Vâta, from that treasure of the immortal which is placed in thy house yonder, give us to live!

Translation by F. Max Müller

I

I magnify Agni, the Purohita, the divine ministrant of the sacrifice, the Hotri priest, the greatest bestower of treasures. Agni, worthy to be magnified by the ancient Rishis and by the present ones—may he conduct the gods hither. May one obtain through Agni wealth and welfare day by day, which may bring glory and high bliss of valiant offspring. Agni, whatever sacrifice and worship thou encompassest on every side, that indeed goes to the gods. May Agni the thoughtful Hotri, he who is true and most splendidly renowned, may the god come hither with the gods. Whatever good thou wilt do to thy worshipper, O Agni, that work verily is thine, O Angiras. Thee, O Agni, we approach day by day, O god who shinest in the darkness; with our prayer, bringing adoration to thee who art the king of all worship, the guardian of Rita, the shining one, increasing in thy own house. Thus, O Agni, be easy of access to us, as a father is to his son. Stay with us for our happiness.

II

We implore with well-spoken words the vigorous Agni who belongs to many people, to the clans that worship the gods, whom other people also magnify. Men have placed Agni on the altar as the augmenter of strength. May we worship thee, rich in sacrificial food. Thus be thou here to-day gracious to us, a helper in our striving for gain, O good one! We choose thee, the all-possessor, as our messenger and as our Hotri. The flames of thee, who art great, spread around; thy rays touch the heaven. The gods, Varuna, Mitra, Aryaman, kindle thee, the ancient messenger. The mortal, O Agni, who worships thee, gains through thee every prize. Thou art the cheerful Hotri and householder, O Agni, the messenger of the clans. In thee all the firm laws are comprised which the gods have made. In thee, the blessed one, O Agni, youngest god, all sacrificial food is offered. Sacrifice then thou who art gracious to us to-day and afterwards, to the gods that we may be rich in valiant men. Him, the king, verily the adorers approach reverentially. With oblations men kindle Agni, having overcome all failures. Destroying the foe, they victoriously got through Heaven and Earth and the waters; they have made wide room for their dwelling. May the manly Agni, after he has received the oblations, become brilliant at the side of Kanva; may he neigh as a horse in battles. Take thy seat; thou art great. Shine forth, thou who most excellently repairest to the gods. O Agni, holy god, emit thy red, beautiful smoke, O glorious one! Thou whom the gods have placed here for Manu as the best performer of the sacrifice, O carrier of oblations, whom Kanva and Medhyâtithi, whom Vrishan and Upastuta have worshipped, the winner of prizes. That Agni's nourishment has shone brightly whom Medhyâtithi and Kanva have kindled on behalf of Rita. Him do these hymns, him do we extol. Fill us with wealth, thou self-dependent one, for thou, O Agni, hast companionship with the gods. Thou art lord over glorious booty. Have mercy upon us; thou art great. Stand up straight for blessing us, like the god Savitri, straight a winner of booty, when we with our worshippers and with ointments call thee in emulation with other people. Standing straight, protect us by thy splendor from evil; burn down every ghoul. Let us stand straight that we may walk and live. Find out our worship among the gods. Save us, O Agni, from the sorcerer, save us from mischief, from the niggard. Save us from him who does us harm or tries to kill us, O youngest god with bright splendor! As with a club smite the niggards in all directions, and him who deceives us, O god with fiery jaws. The mortal who makes his weapons very sharp by night, may that impostor not rule over us. Agni has won abundance in heroes. Agni and the two Mitras have blessed Medhyâtithi. Agni has blessed Upastuta in the acquirement of wealth. Through Agni we call hither from afar Turvasa, Yadu, and Ugradeva. May Agni, our strength against the Dasyu, conduct hither Navavâstva, Brihadratha, and Turvîti.

Manu has established thee, O Agni, as a light for all people. Thou hast shone forth with Kanva, born from Rita, grown strong, thou whom the human races worship. Agni's flames are impetuous and violent; they are terrible and not to be withstood. Always burn down the sorcerers, and the allies of the Yâtus, every ghoul.

III

We choose Agni as our messenger, the all-possessor, as the Hotri of this sacrifice, the highly wise. Agni and Agni! again they constantly invoked with their invocations, the lord of the clans, the bearer of oblations, the beloved of many. Agni, when born, conduct the gods hither for him who has strewn the sacrificial grass; thou art our Hotri, worthy of being magnified. Awaken them, the willing ones, when thou goest as messenger, O Agni. Sit down with the gods on the Barhis. O thou to whom Ghrita oblations are poured out, resplendent god, burn against the mischievous, O Agni, against the sorcerers. By Agni Agni is kindled, the sage, the master of the house, the young one, the bearer of oblations, whose mouth is the sacrificial spoon. Praise Agni the sage, whose ordinances for the sacrifice are true, the god who drives away sickness. Be the protector, O Agni, of a master of sacrificial food who worships thee, O god, as his messenger. Be merciful, O purifier, unto the man who is rich in sacrificial food, and who invites Agni to the feast of the gods. Thus, O Agni, resplendent purifier, conduct the gods hither to us, to our sacrifice and to our food. Thus praised by us with our new Gâyatra hymn, bring us wealth of valiant men and food. Agni with thy bright splendor be pleased, through all our invocations of the gods, with this our praise.

IV

With reverence I shall worship thee who art long-tailed like a horse, Agni, king of worship. May he, our son of strength, proceeding on his broad way, the propitious, become bountiful to us. Thus protect us always, thou who hast a full life, from the mortal who seeks to do us harm, whether near or afar. And mayest thou, O Agni, announce to the gods this our newest efficient Gâyatra song. Let us partake of all booty that is highest and that is middle; help us to the wealth that is nearest. O god with bright splendor, thou art the distributor. Thou instantly flowest for the liberal giver in the wave of the river, near at hand. The mortal, O Agni, whom thou protectest in battles, whom thou speedest in the races, he will command constant nourishment: Whosoever he may be, no one will overtake him, O conqueror Agni! His strength is glorious. May he, known among all tribes, win the race with his horses; may he with the help of his priests become a gainer. O Garâbodha! Accomplish this task for every house: a beautiful song of praise for worshipful Rudra. May he, the great, the immeasurable, the smoke-bannered, rich in splendor, incite us to pious thoughts and to strength. May he hear us, like the rich lord of a clan, the banner of the gods, on behalf of our hymns, Agni with bright light. Reverence to the great ones, reverence to the lesser ones! Reverence to the young, reverence to the old! Let us sacrifice to the gods, if we can. May I not, O gods, fall as a victim to the curse of my better.

Translation by F. Max Müller

V

I press on for you with my prayer to the all-possessing messenger, the immortal bearer of offerings, the best sacrificer. He, the great one, knows indeed the place of wealth, the ascent to heaven; may he conduct the gods hither. He, the god, knows how to direct the gods for the righteous worshipper, in his house. He gives us wealth dear to us. He is the Hotri; he who knows the office of a messenger, goes to and fro, knowing the ascent to heaven. May we be of those who have worshipped Agni with the gift of offerings, who cause him to thrive and kindle him. The men who have brought worship to Agni, are renowned as successful by wealth and by powerful offspring. May much-desired wealth come to us day by day; may gains arise among us. He, the priest of the tribes, the priest of men, pierces all hostile powers by his might as with a tossing bow.

VI

He has brought down the wisdom of many a worshipper, he who holds in his hand all manly power. Agni has become the lord of treasures, he who brought together all powers of immortality. All the clever immortals when seeking did not find the calf though sojourning round about us. The attentive gods, wearying themselves, following his footsteps, stood at the highest, beautiful standing-place of Agni. When the bright ones had done service to thee, the bright one, Agni, with Ghrita through three autumns, they assumed worshipful names; the well-born shaped their own bodies. Acquiring for themselves the two great worlds, the worshipful ones brought forward their Rudra-like powers. The mortal, when beings were in discord, perceived and found out Agni standing in the highest place. Being like-minded they reverentially approached him on their knees. Together with their wives they venerated the venerable one. Abandoning their bodies they made them their own, the one friend waking when the other friend closed his eyes. When the worshipful gods have discovered the thrice seven secret steps laid down in thee, they concordantly guard with them immortality. Protect thou the cattle and that which remains steadfast and that which moves. Knowing, O Agni, the established orders of human dwellings, distribute in due order gifts that they may live. Knowing the ways which the gods do, thou hast become the unwearied messenger, the bearer of oblations. They who knew the right way and were filled with good intentions, beheld from heaven the seven young rivers and the doors of riches. Saramâ found the strong stable of the cows from which human clans receive their nourishment. The Earth has spread herself far and wide with them who are great in their greatness, the mother Aditi, for the refreshment of the bird, with her sons who have assumed all powers of their own dominion, preparing for themselves the way to immortality. When the immortals created the two eyes of heaven, they placed fair splendor in him. Then they rush down like streams let loose. The red ones have recognized, O Agni, those which are directed downwards.

VII

Forward goes your strength tending heavenward, rich in offerings, with the ladle full of ghee. To the gods goes the worshipper desirous of their favor. I magnify with prayer Agni who has knowledge of prayers, the accomplisher of sacrifice, who hears us, and in whom manifold wealth has been laid down. O Agni, may we be able to bridle thee the strong god; may we overcome all hostile powers. Agni, inflamed at the sacrifice, the purifier who should be magnified, whose hair is flame—him we approach with prayers. With his broad stream of light the immortal Agni, clothed in ghee, well served with oblations, is the carrier of offerings at the sacrifice. Holding the sacrificial ladles, performing the sacrifice they have with right thought, pressingly brought Agni hither for help. The Hotri, the immortal god goes in front with his secret power, instigating the sacrifices. The strong is set at the races. He is led forth at the sacrifices, the priest, the accomplisher of sacrifice. He has been produced by prayer, the excellent one. I have established him, the germ of beings, forever the father of Daksha. I have laid thee down, the excellent one, with the nourishment of Daksha, O thou who art produced by power, O Agni, thee the resplendent one, O Usig. The priests, eager to set to work the Rita, kindle with quick strength Agni the governor, him who crosses the waters. I magnify the child of vigor at this sacrifice, who shines under the heaven, the thoughtful Agni. He who should be magnified and adored, who is visible through the darkness, Agni, the manly, is kindled. Agni, the manly, is kindled, he who draws hither the gods like a horse. The worshippers rich in offerings magnify him. We the manly ones will kindle thee the manly god, O manly Agni, who shinest mightily.

VIII

Produce thy stream of flames like a broad onslaught. Go forth impetuous like a king with his elephant, thou art an archer; shoot the sorcerers with thy hottest arrows. Thy whirls fly quickly. Fiercely flaming touch them. O Agni, send forth with the ladle thy heat, thy winged flames; send forth unfettered thy firebrands all around. Being the quickest, send forth thy spies against all evildoers. Be an undeceivable guardian of this clan.

He who attacks us with evil spells, far or near, may no such foe defy thy track. Rise up, O Agni! Spread out against all foes! Burn down the foes, O god with the sharp weapon! When kindled, O Agni, burn down like dry brushwood, the man who exercises malice against us. Stand upright, strike the foes away from us! Make manifest thy divine powers, O Agni! Unbend the strong bows of those who incite demons against us. Crush all enemies, be they relations or strangers. He knows thy favor, O youngest one, who makes a way for a sacred speech like this. Mayest thou beam forth to his doors all auspicious days and the wealth and the splendor of the niggard. Let him, O Agni, be fortunate and blessed with good rain, who longs to gladden thee with constant offerings and hymns through his life in his house. May such longing ever bring auspicious days to him. I praise thy favor; it resounded here. May this song, which is like a favorite wife, awaken for thee. Let us brighten thee, being rich in horses and chariots. Mayest thou maintain our knightly power day by day. May the worshipper here frequently of his own accord approach thee, O god who shinest in darkness, resplendent day by day. Let us worship thee sporting and joyous, surpassing the splendor of other people. Whoever, rich in horses and rich in gold, approaches thee, O Agni, with his chariot full of wealth—thou art the protector and the friend of him who always delights in showing thee hospitality. Through my kinship with thee I break down the great foes by my words. That kinship has come down to me from my father Gotama. Be thou attentive to this our word, O youngest, highly wise Hotri, as the friend of our house. May those guardians of thine, infallible Agni, sitting down together protect us, the never sleeping, onward-pressing, kind, unwearied ones, who keep off the wolf, who never tire. Thy guardians, O Agni, who seeing have saved the blind son of Mamatâ from distress—He the possessor of all wealth has saved them who have done good deeds. The impostors, though trying to deceive, could not deceive. In thy companionship we dwell, protected by

Translation by F. Max Müller

thee. Under thy guidance let us acquire gain. Accomplish both praises, O thou who art the truth! Do so by thy present power, O fearless one! May we worship thee, O Agni, with this log of wood. Accept the hymn of praise which we recite. Burn down those who curse us, the sorcerers. Protect us, O god who art great like Mitra, from guile, from revilement, and from disgrace.

IX

Bright, flaming, like the lover of the Dawn,[8] he has, like the light of the sky, filled the two worlds of Heaven and Earth which are turned towards each other. As soon as thou wert born thou hast excelled by thy power of mind; being the son of the gods thou hast become their father. Agni is a worshipper of the gods, never foolish, always discriminating; he is like the udder of the cows; he is the sweetness of food. Like a kind friend to men, not to be led astray, sitting in the midst, the lovely one, in the house; like a child when born, he is delightful in the house; like a race-horse which is well cared for, he has wandered across the clans. When I call to the sacrifice the clans who dwell in the same nest with the heroes, may Agni then attain all divine powers. When thou hast listened to these heroes, no one breaks those laws of thine. That verily is thy wonderful deed that thou hast killed, with thy companions, all foes; that, joined by the heroes, thou hast accomplished thy works. Like the lover of the Dawn, resplendent and bright, of familiar form: may he thus pay attention to this sacrificer. Carrying him they opened by themselves the doors of heaven. They all shouted at the aspect of the sun.

X

Like unto excellent wealth, like unto the shine of the sun, like unto living breath, like unto one's own son, like unto a quick takvan Agni holds the wood, like milk, like a milch cow, bright and shining. He holds safety, pleasant like a homestead, like ripe barley, a conqueror of men; like a Rishi uttering sacred shouts, praised among the clans; like a well-cared-for race-horse, Agni bestows vigor. He to whose flame men do not grow accustomed, who is like one's own mind, like a wife on a couch, enough for all happiness. When the bright Agni has shone forth, he is like a white horse among people, like a chariot with golden ornaments, impetuous in fights. Like an army which is sent forward he shows his vehemence, like an archer's shaft with sharp point. He who is born is one twin; he who will be born is the other twin—the lover of maidens, the husband of wives. As cows go to their stalls, all that moves and we, for the sake of a dwelling, reach him who has been kindled. Like the flood of the Sindhu he has driven forward the downward-flowing waters. The cows lowed at the sight of the sun.

XI

The Hotri goes forward in order to fulfil his duty by his wonderful power, directing upwards the brightly adorned prayer. He steps towards the sacrificial ladles which are turned to the right, and which first kiss his foundation. They have greeted with shouts the streams of Rita which were hidden at the birthplace of the god, at his seat. When He dwelt dispersed in the lap of the waters, he drank the draughts by the power of which he moves. Two beings of the same age try to draw that wonderful shape

Translation by F. Max Müller

towards themselves, progressing in turns towards a common aim.
Then he is to be proclaimed by us like a winner in a contest. The
charioteer governs all things as if pulling in the reins of a
draught-horse. He whom two beings of the same age serve, two
twins dwelling together in one common abode, the gray one has
been born as a youth by night as by day, the ageless one who
wanders through many generations of men. The prayers, the ten
fingers stir him up. We, the mortals, call him, the god, for his
protection. From the dry land he hastens to the declivities. With
those who approached him he has established new rules. Thou
indeed, O Agni, reignest by thy own nature over the heavenly
and over the terrestrial world as a shepherd takes care of his
cattle. These two variegated, great goddesses striving for
gloriousness, the golden ones who move crookedly, have
approached thy sacrificial grass. Agni! Be gratified and accept
graciously this prayer, O joy-giver, independent one, who art
born in the Rita, good-willed one, whose face is turned towards
us from all sides, conspicuous one, gay in thy aspect, like a
dwelling-place rich in food.

Footnote 8:   The sun.

16585909R00035

Printed in Poland
by Amazon Fulfillment
Poland Sp. z o.o., Wrocław